the MINDFULNESS effect

JOURNAL & PRACTICE PLANNER

DENA SAMUELS, PhD

NIGHT RIVER PRESS

The Mindfulness Effect: An unexpected journey to healing, connection, and social justice.

Copyright © 2018 Dena Samuels PhD.

All rights reserved. No part of this publication may be reproduced, distributed, or transmitted in any form or by any means, including photocopying, recording, or other electronic or mechanical methods, without the prior written permission of the publisher, except in the case of brief quotations embodied in critical reviews and certain other noncommercial uses permitted by copyright law. For permission requests, write to the publisher, addressed "Attention: Permissions Coordinator," at the address below.

ISBN (Paperback): 978-1-7324836-0-6
ISBN (eBook): 978-1-7324836-1-3
ISBN (Audio Book): 978-1-7324836-2-0
ISBN (Journal): 978-1-7324836-3-7

Library of Congress Control Number: 2018949101

Front cover image: Dena Samuels PhD
Book & cover design: Matthew LaFleur

First printing edition 2018.

Samuels, Dena
    The mindfulness effect: an unexpected journey to healing, connection, and social justice / Dena Samuels
    p. cm.

Publisher Night River Press
Denver, CO, 80209
www.nightriverpress.com

Other books by author:
The Culturally Inclusive Educator: Preparing for a Multicultural World
(Teachers College Press, 2014)
The Matrix Reader: Examining the Dynamics of Oppression and Privilege
(McGraw-Hill, 2009)

Welcome to *The Mindfulness Effect* Journal & Practice Planner!

This book can help you take your mindfulness practice to the next level, and make it your own. Journaling can assist in furthering your mindfulness journey by providing the space to document your experience. By taking the time to reflect on your experience, you gain the opportunity to access deep insights you might otherwise have missed.

Journaling is the first step to unlocking your unlimited potential for healing, self-empowerment, culturally inclusive leadership, social and environmental justice. It is also important to make a plan to progress on your journey. Consider how you'd like to incorporate mindfulness in your life.

The titles of each mindfulness practice and activity from *The Mindfulness Effect* are provided here for your convenience. For each one, take the opportunity to journal whatever emotions, ideas, thoughts, insights, shifts, etc. arise in you.

After your reflection of each guided meditation, you will then have the opportunity to consider how deeply each practice resonated with you. You'll know it's a good fit if it speaks to you in some way – if it leaves you feeling moved, or motivated, or just plain good. Ask yourself: Did it provide a shift in my perception? A shift in my emotional or physical state? Did it provide insight that is useful to me? Was it a practice I would like or be willing to repeat, even if it was challenging to me? On a scale of 1-10, you will be given the chance to rate each practice in terms of if you would like to incorporate it into your regular mindfulness plan.

After going through all the mindfulness practices and activities offered in *The Mindfulness Effect*, you will have a better idea of which practices you are more drawn to, and will be prepared to create your own mindfulness plan using those specific practices. Towards the end of this book, you will have the space to create your plan.

This is your journey, and your practice. Make it your own.

With unending peace and connection,
Dena Samuels, PhD
The Mindfulness Effect (Night River Press, 2018)

INTRODUCTION: What is Mindful Liberation?

In this moment, there is plenty of time. In this moment, you are precisely as you should be. In this moment, there is infinite possibility.

~Victoria Moran

REFLECTIONS FROM MINDFULNESS PRACTICE 1:
PRESENT MOMENT/FINDING STILLNESS/FOCUSING ON THE BREATH

On a scale of 1-10, how much did this practice resonate with you? _____

**REFLECTIONS FROM MINDFULNESS PRACTICE 2:
LEAF ON A STREAM/CLOUD IN THE SKY**

On a scale of 1-10, how much did this practice resonate with you? _____

CHAPTER 1: Social Conditioning – Living from the Outside In

"Our limited perceptions get in the way of our greatness"
~Dr. Shakti Butler

REFLECTIONS FROM MINDFULNESS PRACTICE 3: THE OBSERVER

_____

_____

_____

_____

_____

_____

_____

_____

_____

_____

_____

_____

_____

_____

_____

_____

_____

On a scale of 1-10, how much did this practice resonate with you? _____

**REFLECTIONS FROM MINDFULNESS PRACTICE 4:
UNPACKING OUR STORIES**

On a scale of 1-10, how much did this practice resonate with you? _____

**REFLECTIONS FROM MINDFULNESS PRACTICE 5:
FINDING YOUR GIFTS**

On a scale of 1-10, how much did this practice resonate with you? _____

CHAPTER 2: Who/What We Really Are – Living from the Inside Out

"When you live from the inside out, it doesn't matter how chaotic the world around you is. You're at peace with yourself."
~Assegid Habtewold

**REFLECTIONS FROM MINDFULNESS PRACTICE 6:
WE ARE MORE THAN THE BODIES THAT HOLD US**

On a scale of 1-10, how much did this practice resonate with you? _____

CHAPTER 3: Mindfulness in Context and Spiritual Bypassing

You are an extension of me. You are not separate from me. When I see you, I see myself. When I see you, I see my light reflected in your light.

~Ubuntu

REFLECTIONS FROM MINDFULNESS PRACTICE 7: EXPANDING YOUR LIGHT/CONNECTING WITH COMMUNITY

On a scale of 1-10, how much did this practice resonate with you? _____

Taking A Privilege Inventory

On a scale of 1-10, how much did this practice resonate with you? _____

CHAPTER 4: Mindfulness to Discover the Wisdom Our Bodies Hold

"The way to your spirit is through your body." ~Ashley Asti

**REFLECTIONS FROM MINDFULNESS PRACTICE 8:
FROM REACTION TO RESPONSE: CULTIVATING OPENHEARTEDNESS**

On a scale of 1-10, how much did this practice resonate with you? _____

CHAPTER 5: Mindful Liberation

"Right here in our bodies, in our defense of our right to experience joy, in the refusal to abandon the place where we have been most completely invaded and colonized, in our determination to make the bombed and defoliated lands flower again and bear fruit, here where we have been most shamed is one of the most radical and sacred places from which to transform the world."
~Aurora Levins Morales

REFLECTIONS FROM MINDFULNESS PRACTICE 9: EMBODIED HEALING

On a scale of 1-10, how much did this practice resonate with you? _____

CHAPTER 6: Mindfully Living "On Purpose" – Finding Your Purpose for a Meaningful Life

"When the higher incorporates the lower into its service, the nature of the lower is transformed into that of the higher." ~Eckhart Tolle

**REFLECTIONS FROM MINDFULNESS PRACTICE 10:
FINDING YOUR PURPOSE: GETTING STILL, ASKING, AND LISTENING**

On a scale of 1-10, how much did this practice resonate with you? _____

**REFLECTIONS FROM MINDFULNESS PRACTICE 11:
IMAGINE! DREAM BIG!**

Your Desire Inventory

- *What do I want?*

- *How am I meant to manifest my highest purpose?*

- *How can I move toward my goals with maximum joy in my life?*

- *What might my best life look like?*

- *What might my best life feel like?*

On a scale of 1-10, how much did this practice resonate with you? _____

Setting Intentions

- *What are some possible intentions that might mean living a more expansive life than the one I am currently living?*

- *What is one action I could take to help make one of my dreams/desires come true?*

CHAPTER 7: Mindfully Discovering What Stops Us

"Sometimes it's the journey that teaches you a lot about your destination."
~Drake

**REFLECTIONS FROM MINDFULNESS PRACTICE 12:
BREAKING FREE FROM DOUBT**

On a scale of 1-10, how much did this practice resonate with you? _____

Limiting Beliefs Inventory

• *What are some limiting beliefs or messages I've learned about myself that stop me from living my best life?*

**REFLECTIONS FROM MINDFULNESS PRACTICE 13:
CHALLENGING OUR LIMITING BELIEFS**

On a scale of 1-10, how much did this practice resonate with you? _____

CHAPTER 8: Going Deeper – Mindfully Staying on Track

"Life's challenges are not supposed to paralyze you; they're supposed to help you discover who you are." ~Bernice Johnson Reagon

Reflections on Gardner's Life Mapping

REFLECTIONS FROM MINDFULNESS PRACTICE 14: ROOT TO RISE

On a scale of 1-10, how much did this practice resonate with you? _____

**REFLECTIONS FROM MINDFULNESS PRACTICE 15:
FINDING GRATITUDE**

On a scale of 1-10, how much did this practice resonate with you? _____

CHAPTER 9: What Stops Us from Building Relationships Across Difference

To overcome our biases, we must walk boldly towards them. ~Verne Myers

Reflections on Acknowledging Your Socialization

REFLECTIONS FROM MINDFULNESS PRACTICE 16: CONNECTING WITH EXCLUSION AND EMPOWERING OURSELVES

On a scale of 1-10, how much did this practice resonate with you? _____

**REFLECTIONS FROM MINDFULNESS PRACTICE 17:
CHALLENGING OUR ASSUMPTIONS**

On a scale of 1-10, how much did this practice resonate with you? _____

REFLECTIONS FROM MINDFULNESS PRACTICE 18: SUCCESSFULLY INTERRUPTING MICROAGGRESSIONS

On a scale of 1-10, how much did this practice resonate with you? _____

CHAPTER 10: Mindfulness for Cultural Inclusion – Connecting Across Differences

"It is not our differences that divide us. It is our inability to recognize, accept, and celebrate those differences." ~Audre Lorde

Relationship Inventory

**REFLECTIONS FROM MINDFULNESS PRACTICE 19:
CONNECTING THE SPIRITUAL WITH THE PHYSICAL**

On a scale of 1-10, how much did this practice resonate with you? _____

**REFLECTIONS FROM MINDFULNESS PRACTICE 20:
METTA/LOVINGKINDNESS**

On a scale of 1-10, how much did this practice resonate with you? _____

CHAPTER 11: Mindfulness for Social Justice

"Let us be the ancestors our descendants will thank." ~Winona LaDuke

**REFLECTIONS FROM MINDFULNESS PRACTICE 21:
ACKNOWLEDGING THE IMPACT OF AN UNFAIR SYSTEM**

On a scale of 1-10, how much did this practice resonate with you? _____

**REFLECTIONS FROM MINDFULNESS PRACTICE 22:
CHOOSING TO MAKE A DIFFERENCE**

On a scale of 1-10, how much did this practice resonate with you? _____

Mindful Action Inventory

CHAPTER 12: Mindfully Connecting Social Justice & Environmental Justice

"We live in an interconnected world, in an interconnected time, and we need holistic solutions. We have a crisis of inequality, and we need climate solutions that solve that crisis." ~Naomi Klein

REFLECTIONS FROM MINDFULNESS PRACTICE 23: INTERCONNECTEDNESS

On a scale of 1-10, how much did this practice resonate with you? _____

**REFLECTIONS FROM MINDFULNESS PRACTICE 24:
IMPACT ON THE EARTH**

On a scale of 1-10, how much did this practice resonate with you? _____

Reflections on Our Sanctuary Within

- *What are some of the practices I might incorporate in my own life, such as mindful consumption, mindful eating, mindful movement, health/wellness?*

CONCLUSION: Takeaways

Ubuntu means I am because we are.

REFLECTIONS FROM MINDFULNESS PRACTICE 25: LIVING AN INSPIRED LIFE

On a scale of 1-10, how much did this practice resonate with you? _____

Mindfulness Practice Planner

Congratulations on finishing the practices and activities in *The Mindfulness Effect*! You are now ready to make the practice your own!

Take some time to review your journal entries, and especially your scores at the end of each mindful meditation. Which practices were you more drawn to than others? Which would help you achieve all that you want to so you can take your life, your organization, and the world to the next level?

Here's your chance to create a plan for yourself to guide you moving forward. Consider these questions as you brainstorm the ways you can incorporate mindfulness in your life:

What is your intention for incorporating mindfulness in your life? What do you hope to gain from beginning or expanding your practice?

_____

_____

_____

_____

_____

_____

_____

_____

_____

_____

_____

_____

_____

How often do you plan to practice mindfulness? Daily? Twice/day? Every time you're waiting in line? When you're in traffic? When you're brushing your teeth?

What might your practice entail? Daily seated meditation? Walking meditation? Focusing on your breath at certain times during the day? Taking a conscious breath before interacting with others? Journaling? Other contemplative practices?

What are some obstacles that might keep you from continuing your mindfulness plan?

How will you get yourself back on track when life/Conditioned Self gets in the way?

What might you bring into your life that will bring you joy along your path? What fun activities might you incorporate more into your life so you don't take yourself/your life/this plan too seriously?

How might you use mindfulness in your place of work? How will you use mindfulness as a tool to connect deeply with others?

How might mindful leadership be an asset to your workplace for your organization, corporation, campus, school, etc. to excel?

How might you use mindfulness to create a more sustainable way of living?

How can you connect with others on mindfulness to share ideas, thoughts, insights? Are there people in your life (friends, family, co-workers, etc.) with whom you would like to share your journey? If so, name them.

Once you have used these questions to help you brainstorm your Mindfulness Practice Planner, choose at least one answer from each question to begin to formulate a plan you can begin to implement today. Write out your plan below. Once you take a step in the direction you want to head, ideas and insight will show up everywhere! Continue to add them to this plan as you go.

And remember, you are not alone on this journey. Please take advantage of the following opportunities to connect and deepen your practice, and to get support as you go:

- Download or stream all 25 mindfulness practices offered in *The Mindfulness Effect* for FREE!

- Join The Mindfulness Effect Facebook Community to connect with others about your mindfulness journey: ask questions, receive guidance, share experiences, and learn more;

- Sign up for The Mindfulness Effect Online Course to deepen your practice and gain further insight from the author;

- Sign up for our newsletter and blogs;

- Learn more about the services Dena Samuels Consulting offers (mindfulness-based diversity, equity, and inclusion keynotes, workshops, Lunch&Learns, strategic planning, executive and personal coaching, and more!)

FOR INFO ON ALL THESE OPTIONS, VISIT: WWW.DENASAMUELS.COM

www.ingramcontent.com/pod-product-compliance
Lightning Source LLC
Chambersburg PA
CBHW071026080526
44587CB00015B/2512